300
Incredible
Things for Golfers
on the
Internet

300INCREDIBLE.COM, LLC
600 Village Trace, Building 23
Marietta, Georgia 30067

(800) 909-6505

Printed in China

ISBN 0-9658668-3-1

Introduction

This book was written for all those people who love life on "the links." The Internet is full of links that will help you pursue your passion when off the golf course. You'll find an amazing array of Web sites that will educate, entertain and inform you all about the wonderful world of golf. So, keep your head down, eyes on the monitor, a firm grip on the mouse and follow through.

Ken Leebow
Leebow@300INCREDIBLE.COM
http://www.300INCREDIBLE.COM

About the Author

Ken Leebow has been involved with the computer business for over twenty years. The Internet has fascinated him since he began exploring it several years ago, and he has helped over a million readers utilize its resources. Ken has appeared frequently in the media, educating individuals about the Web's greatest hits. He is considered a leading expert on what is incredible about the Internet.

When not online, you can find Ken playing tennis, running, reading or spending time with his family. He is living proof that being addicted to the Net doesn't mean giving up on the other pleasures of life.

— Dedication —

To my dad, who lives and loves the game of golf.
He taught me so much about the sport...such as
don't throw your club after a lousy shot.

Acknowledgments

Putting a book together requires many expressions of appreciation. I do this with great joy, as there are several people who have played vital roles in the process:

- My kids, Alissa and Josh, who helped identify some of the cool sites.

- My wife, Denice, who has been patient with me while I have spent untold hours on the Internet.

- Paul Joffe and Janet Bolton, of *TBI Creative Services*, for their editing and graphics skills and for keeping me focused.

- The multitude of great people who have encouraged and assisted me via e-mail.

- Mark Krasner and Janice Caselli for sharing my vision of the book and helping make it a reality.

The Incredible Internet Book Series

300 Incredible Things to Do on the Internet

300 More Incredible Things to Do on the Internet

300 Incredible Things for Kids on the Internet

300 Incredible Things for Sports Fans on the Internet

300 Incredible Things for Golfers on the Internet

300 Incredible Things for Travelers on the Internet

300 Incredible Things for Health, Fitness & Diet on the Internet

300 Incredible Things for Auto Racing Fans on the Internet

300 Incredible Things for Self-Help & Wellness on the Internet

300 Incredible Things to Learn on the Internet

300 Incredible Things for Home Improvement on the Internet

300 Incredible Things for Seniors on the Internet

300 Incredible Things for Pet Lovers on the Internet

300 Incredible Things for Women on the Internet

America Online Web Site Directory
Where to Go for What You Need

TABLE OF CONTENTS

TABLE OF CONTENTS (continued)

CHAPTER I
BEST OF THE BEST

1
Golf Online

http://www.golfonline.com

The publishers of Golf Magazine and Golf Week will keep you current.

2
Golf.com

http://www.golf.com

Fore, score and the Internet. Everything you ever needed to know about golf is at this site.

3
GolfWeb

http://www.golfweb.com
The folks from Sportsline know how to cover golf.

4
Golf Weekly

http://www.golfweek.com
Weekly, go long and deep into the news, scores and other golf information with this award-winning magazine.

5
The World of Golf

http://www.worldgolf.com
The world of golf comes alive with current and timely information.

6
Get on the Circuit

http://www.golfcircuit.com

If you can't play on the circuit, you can at least get tips, humor and a bunch of other good things at this site.

7
Tune In to the Golf Channel

http://www.thegolfchannel.com

What's on the tube? Statistics and a "hole" lot more.

8
Ain't Golf Great?

http://www.greatgolf.com

Great courses, tournament information, weather, news and more.

9
Excited About Golf

http://sports.excite.com/pga
Search engines are almost as popular as golf. You can tell Excite loves golf.

10
Yahoo Wants You…

http://sports.yahoo.com/pga
…to know a lot about golf.

11
Golf Stories

http://www.zooba.com
Sign up for the golf mailing list at Zooba. Each e-mail will inform, entertain and provide a historical perspective about golf.

12
Snap to It!

http://www.snap.com
Snap, one of the Web portal sites, has an excellent golf site. When you arrive, click on the golf section.

13
ESPN Knows Golf

http://espn.go.com/golfonline
One of the best sports sites on the Net has tons of information for golf fans.

14
Golf Illustrated

http://www.cnnsi.com/golf
http://www.golfillustrated.com
Let CNNSI and Golf Illustrated give you the scoop about golf.

15

USA Today

http://www.usatoday.com/sports/golf/sg.htm

The USA's national paper covers our national obsession.

16

Times for Golf

http://www.nytimes.com/yr/mo/day/sports/golf

The New York Times has in-depth reporting about the golf industry.

17

The Post Knows Golf

http://www.washingtonpost.com/wp-dyn/sports/leaguesandsports/golf

Let the paper from the Nation's Capital keep you up-to-date about golf.

18
The Sports Network

http://www.tsn.ca/golf
Get information and TV schedules for all the major tours.

19
Golf Digest

http://www.golfdigest.com
GolfDigest says: "How to play, what to play, where to play." Can't beat that.

20
Fox Sports

http://www.foxsports.com/golf
Tune in to the Fox network for scores and more.

21
Information That Hits the Mark

http://www.infobeat.com

InfoBeat will e-mail you very timely golf information. Make sure you click sports and golf.

22
Golf Network

http://www.sportsnetwork.com

The Sports Network has current golf information and stats. Hit the golf link and let it rip.

23
LA Golf

http://sports.latimes.com/gol/gol

The LA Times has complete reporting and statistics for all the major tours.

24
Serve Up Golf
http://www.sportserver.com
Timely golf reporting with all the majors covered in great detail.

25
You Wanna Bet?
http://www.sporting-life.com/golf/news
http://www.sporting-life.com/betting/golf/news
Sporting Life has current news, but you might also want to check out the betting and odds site.

26
Feed Me the Information
http://www.sportsfeed.com/golf
Timely and detailed golf information await you here.

27
Golf on the Web
http://uk.sports.com/golf/index.html
Sports Web will keep you current with golf news. You can even sign up for a golf newsletter here.

28
Through The Years
http://www.infoplease.com/ipsa/A0110156.html
There are historical stats galore at this site.

29
The Answer Is
http://www.askjeeves.com
Ask Jeeves a golf question, and he will guide you to the answer.

30
Golf Radio
http://www.thegolfshow.com
Listen to helpful information from the Golf Radio Network.

31
Stay Tuned
http://www.gist.com/prepack/interzine/igolf
If you can't be on the links or on the Net, you might want to see what's on TV about golf.

32
Listen Up
http://www.broadcast.com/sports/golf
If you want to listen to golf broadcasts on the Net, here's your spot.

33
Kids Know Golf History

http://library.advanced.org/10556/english/high/history/index.htm

This library has been established to help kids design Web sites, and this particular site focuses on the history of golf.

CHAPTER II
THE TOUR AND MORE

34
Gentlemen's Golf

http://www.pga.com
Here's the official site of the PGA. One of the finest golf sites on the Net.

35
Ladies' Golf

http://www.lpga.com
The official site for the LPGA. Lots of great information here.

36
It's the Equipment

http://www.golfweb.com/equipment/proreport/index.html
Before you buy your next set of clubs, find out what the winning pros are using on the tour.

"What would I like for my birthday?
Well, I could use a golf bag."

37
The Majors
http://www.worldgolf.com/tournaments/majors
The Masters, The U.S. Open, The British Open, The PGA Championship—I can hear the roar of the fans as the players approach the 18th green.

38
The British Open
http://www.opengolf.com
http://www.britishopen.net
These Web sites are open for you.

39
Who's the Best?
http://www.worldseriesofgolf.com
The World Series of golf helps determine the best in the game.

40
PGA Championship

http://www.pga.com/tour

Details about the PGA Championship. And if you're interested in attending the tournament, get your tickets here.

41
The Ryder Cup

http://www.rydercup.com

Who is the best of all? This international competition answers that question.

42
The Masters

http://www.masters.org
http://www.augustagolf.com

Go for the green jacket.

43
The Open

http://www.usopen.com
The official site for the U.S. Open.

44
The Seniors Open

http://www.1999senioropen.com
http://www.2000senioropen.com
http://www.2001senioropen.com
Details of the U.S. Senior Open for 1999, 2000 and beyond.

45
Golf Scoring and Information System

http://www.unisys.com/Sports/Golf/SeniorOpen98/Clubhouse.ASP?PG=02&ID=01
How they track the scores is pretty interesting.

46
What's Goin' on in Europe?
http://www.europeantour.com
The European Tour has many great golfers. Check them out here.

47
The Asian Tour
http://www.asianpgatour.com
See what's happening in the Orient.

48
What's in Your Future?
http://www.futurestour.com
The Futures Tour is the country's leading developmental tour for women's professional golf.

49
Club Nike

http://www.nikegolfclub.com

Here's a golf club that you can join for free. If you're a fan of Nike, go ahead and become a member.

50
Acura World of Golf

http://www.worldofgolftv.com

It has nice cars and a great Web site for you to keep up with the golf world.

51
World Ice Golf Championship

http://www.greenland-guide.gl/gt/icegolf/default.htm

Whether you have ever enjoyed a good game of "ice golf" or not, visit this site from Greenland.

CHAPTER III
WHO'S WHO IN SPIKES

52
Pros Online

http://www.rayfloyd.com
http://www.bencrenshaw.com
http://www.phil-mickelson.com
http://www.woosie.com
Not many pro golfers have their own Web sites. Here are a few that do.

53
Thank You Chi Chi

http://www.chichi.org
The Chi Chi Rodriguez Youth Foundation, Inc.'s mission is to serve inner city youths—who are at risk of dropping out of school—by improving their self-esteem, character, work ethic, social adjustment and academic performance.

54
Jose Maria Olazabal
http://www.aboutgolf.com/jmo
It's all about Jose!

55
Tiger Woods
http://www.tigerwoods.com
http://www.websites2000.com/golf/twoods
These sites (and Tiger himself) should be around for a long time. Check out the guy who has given golf a big shot in the arm.

56
Tiger Fans Unite
http://www.clubtiger.com
If you love Tiger, join his fan club.

57
Take Stock
http://www.golfinvestors.com
You love to watch them play; why not invest in them, too?

58
Get a Grip
http://www.gripitandripit.com
The controversial John Daily maintains his official Web site here.

59
Da Bear
http://www.nicklaus.com
Jack Nicklaus goes high tech on the Web. If you like Jack, you'll enjoy this site.

60
The World of Gary Player

http://www.garyplayer.com
Gary is very Web savvy. At his site you can learn all about him or buy some of his products.

61
Arnie's Army

http://www.arnoldpalmer.com
Biographical info about Arnold Palmer is featured at this site.

62
Arnie's the Man

http://www.apga.com
Even if you don't attend the Arnold Palmer Golf Academy, you'll enjoy this site.

63
The Shark
http://www.shark.com
Watch out for Greg Norman. His official Web site will give you everything you ever wanted to know about him.

64
David Duval
http://www.geocities.com/Augusta/7975
While David doesn't yet have an official site, this site fills in very nicely.

65
I'm Famous
http://www.biography.com
Type in a famous player's name, and get his biography.

66
Biography.men
http://pgatour.com/players
http://espn.go.com/golfonline/tours/pga/profiles/index.html
Learn a little more about the men on the tour. Here are their bios.

67
Biography.ladies
http://www.lpga.com/tour/players/bios/bios.html
Learn a little more about the ladies on the tour. Here are their bios.

68
Biography.seniors
http://www.golfweb.com/players/index.html
Learn a little more about the senior golfers.

69
The Hall of Fame

http://www.wgv.com

Visit the World Golf Village, and learn about some of the traditions and all-time great golfers.

CHAPTER IV
TEE TIME

70
St. Andrews

http://www.standrews.org.uk
http://www.standrewsgolf.com
Visit the granddaddy of 'em all.

71
Links, Links, Links

http://www.linksmagazine.com
From the greatest holes in the world to golf travel, you'll find it all here.

"My husband's a doctor. I made the mistake of telling
him I wanted to spend more time together. Now I
caddy three times a week."

72
Golfcourse Plus

http://www.golfcourse.com
http://courseguide.golfweb.com
Need to know a little more about a golf course? These sites tell all.

73
Going Public

http://www.golfpublic.com
Which public courses are the best? Find out here.

74
Serve Me a Course

http://www.golfserv.com
Select a course by a variety of different criteria—price, location, public, private and more.

75
Passport to Courses
http://www.golferspassport.com

"Without question, it's the best deal in golf today." That's what it says at Hale Irwin's Golfers' Passport. For a small yearly membership fee, you can play all of Passport's golf courses without paying green fees.

76
Golf on the Cheap
http://www.golfathalfprice.com

We all know golf can be a bit expensive. If you want to save a little money, pay a visit to this site.

77
Time for Tee
http://www.thegolfer.com

The time has almost come to schedule your tee times through the Net.

78
Sign Me Up

http://www.teemaster.com
Make your tee time online here.

79
Golf Now

http://www.golfnow.com
Search over 17,000 courses and book a tee time with a participating course.

80
Play Golf Now

http://www.playgolfnow.com
No argument from me. This site claims to have 180,000 members and will provide you with discounts at various golf courses.

81
Coupon Please

http://www.golfcpons.com

Couponing is a hobby for many, and golf coupons can save you money at courses located throughout the United States.

82
Work Golf

http://www.usgolfjobs.com

If you love being on the links, maybe you should find a job in the industry.

83
Picture This

http://golf.traveller.com/golf/scorecards

This site has actual course layouts. It doesn't have all 15,000 courses, but you'll find many of them here.

84
Guide Me to a Course

http://www.golfguide.com
Just click on a location map and find out about courses in that area.

85
Play the Best

http://www.golfonline.com/travel
http://www.golfonline.com/travel/resorts/profiler/index.html
America's best courses are ranked and listed here. And use the resort profiler to find the resort that meets your needs.

86
Yahoo!, Let's Play Golf

http://sports.yahoo.com/pga/golfcourses
The folks at Yahoo! list many golf courses for you.

87
Wanna Play a Round?

http://www.play18.com

This site will let you find so many courses that you just might play 36.

88
Golf Weather

http://www.weather.com/golf

Is the sun shining on you today? Before you hit the links, check out the weather. Lots of goodies for you here.

CHAPTER V
FUN WITHOUT CLUBS

89
CyberGolf

http://www.cybergolf.com
Trivia, golf courses and other fun stuff.

90
Golf IQ

http://www.mygolf.com/iqtest
Are you a smart golfer? Take the test and find out.

91
Bogey

http://www.pga.com/FAQ/trivia_02.html
Where did that term come from? I think you'll be surprised. Find that out and much more at this site.

92
Trivia Golf

http://www.triviagolf.com

http://www.golftrivia.com

If you are a golf fan, these are fun trivia sites you will not want to miss. Here's a sample: "Who was the modern era player to come closest to winning all of the Grand Slam events in one year? Answer: Ben Hogan."

93
Caddyshack

http://www.carlspackler.com

http://us.imdb.com/Title?Caddyshack+(1980)

Everything you ever wanted to know about the movie.

94
Tin Cup
http://www.movies.warnerbros.com/tincup
No Kevin Costner here, but there is some fun golf stuff.

95
I'm Thinking of You
http://www.123greetings.com/sports
Go ahead, send a golf greeting card to one of your buddies or family members.

96
You Can Quote Me
http://www.worldseriesofgolf.com/jokes
Funny golf quotes from famous people you know.

97
Joke A Day

http://www.dailygolfjokes.com
Get a good golf joke e-mailed to you every day.

98
Handicap Blues

http://www.badgolfmonthly.com
They say it best: "The online magazine for the golfer whose handicap is golf."

99
Wall Street Meets Golf

http://www.wallstreetsports.com
This site operates a stock market simulation where pro golfers have been transformed into securities.

100
What's the Value?

http://www.parvalu.com

ParValu is "Dow Jones" of the golf world. Happy investing.

101
What's Your Fantasy?

http://www.sportsline.commissioner.com

http://pga.fantasyteam.com

http://www.golfweek.com/fantasy

Fantasy baseball started it all. Now you can play fantasy golf.

102
Toon Time

http://www.chaseoaks.com/cartoon.html

Sometimes you just gotta laugh at our game.

103
Bad Golfers Unite
http://www.badgolf.com
Not you, of course. But here, all the bad golfers of the world can stand up and be counted.

104
Golf and Beer
http://guzzler.cybertude.com
For the golfer who brings along a six-pack.

105
Look It Up
http://www.worldgolf.com/wglibrary/reference/dictionary
Ever wonder what some of those weird golf terms mean? Wonder no more!

106
Business Through Golf

http://www.bizgolf.com
Maximize your bottom line through golf: Sounds like a lofty goal to me.

107
8000 to 1

http://www.worldgolf.com/holeinone/index.html
Those are the odds of making a hole-in-one. If you've already made one,
register it with World Golf to let everyone know.

108
Think Golf

http://library.advanced.org/10556
A bunch of smart kids have created this must-see golf site that is full of
interesting things.

"Do you want me to get you a passport in case you hit China?"

109
My Golf Course Pencil Collection
http://users.erols.com/golferjim
This guy collects golf course pencils. I'm sure you have a few extras to send.

110
Ball Collection
http://www.cu-online.com/~klharney
Check out those balls!

111
Score Card Collection
http://hometown.aol.com/bcat520/golf.html
Don't throw away your scorecards. People collect them.

112
Frisbee Golf

http://www.discgolf.com
http://www.pdga.com
Okay, so this isn't golf with a club, but it still takes a lot of skill to play it.

113
Golf Postcards

http://www.cartoonpostcards.com/golfcards.html
Ed Cleary has many funny cartoons for you. Buy a pack and send them to all your golfing buddies.

114
He's a Maniac

http://www.thegolfmaniac.com/jokes.htm
Actually, he's just your average hacker who loves the game of golf.

115
Nuts About Golf

http://www.golfnuts.com
Let's face it, you wouldn't have this book if you weren't nuts about golf. So go ahead, check out the society.

116
Backyard Putting Green

http://www.ampacseed.com/putgreen.htm
Before you build your own putting green, find out what it takes.

117
Speed It Up

http://www.speedgolf.com
Are you tired of playing golf in the slow lane? Learn about the exciting sport of Speed Golf.

118
Extreme Golf

http://www.extremegolf.com
Whoever said you don't really get much exercise when playing golf should go to this site and get extreme.

119
Golf Balls

http://www.myballs.com
How do you make the subject of golf balls interesting and funny? This site has the answer.

120
Link Me Up

http://www.golflink.com
From associations to tournaments, you'll get a lot of good stuff from this self-proclaimed "premier web guide."

121
WWWGolfer.com
http://www.yougogolf.com
The history of golf, rants, links and other stuff await you at this fan site.

122
Meet the Duffers
http://www.halcyon.com/duffers
Follow the misadventures of "The Duffers" as they travel the fairways of life at the Gopher Hole & Country Club.

123
The Hacker
http://www.golf.ph
"We don't belong to country clubs and walk instead of ride. The ball we play? 'Twas on sale today. That's how we decide."

124
Join Jack on Tour
http://www.jacknickonlinetour.com
It's an online multiplayer game. If you enjoy playing golf on the Net, you might want to ante up the bucks to play.

125
Rules We Hate
http://www.golfonline.com/rules/hatedrules/story1098.html
Golf rules can be weird and obscure. Here are the ones that we really hate.

126
Know Thy Rules
http://www.golfrules.com
You can buy the book here or take an interesting quiz about the rules.

127
You've Got Balls
http://www.savingsolutions.com/ballinformation.html
Everything you ever wanted to know about golf balls but never asked.

128
Golf Clip Art
http://www.savingsolutions.com/clipart.html
If you're building a golf Web site, this might come in handy.

129
Poetry in Motion
http://www.golfpoet.com
You gotta love anyone who writes a book of golf poems.

130
Nothing But Golf

http://www.nothingbutgolf.com
Lots of interesting and fun information for you.

131
Country Club.com

http://www.countryclubs.com
Fortunately, this one is free. If you need a golf dictionary, you'll find it here.

132
Talk About Golf

http://www.deja.com
http://www.liszt.com
What are folks talking about in regard to golf? Go here, type in "golf" and you will be propelled into the world of newsgroups.

133
The Lighter Side
http://www.geocities.com/Augusta/4827/frames.html
If you had a bad round, hang out here for a few chuckles.

134
Whole Golf
http://hamegg.rivals.com
Get honest opinions about golf and equipment from a couple of guys named Ham and Egg.

135
Wow Putter
http://www.heyhon.com/wow/putter.html
The putter that has everything…for the golfer who has everything.

136
Game Guide
http://www.digitalsports.com/golf.html
Digital Sports previews and reviews many popular electronic golf games.

137
Microsoft Golf
http://www.microsoft.com/sports/golf
If you can't get outside and play today, you can download this popular computer golf game now.

138
Chat Golf
http://www.broadcast.com/Sports_Events/Golf
There are many chat rooms on the Net dedicated to golf. Go ahead, chat with your golf buddies.

CHAPTER VI
IMPROVE YOUR GAME

139
Better Golf

http://www.golflink.com/tips/index.shtml

From the basics to the mental aspect, you'll find tips here for every part of your game.

140
Mr. Etiquette

http://www.mrgolf.com

Mr. Golf knows the etiquette of the game. Do you?

141

Learn To...

http://www.learn2.com/08/0814/0814.html

...putt!

142

The Amateur Golfer Advisor

http://www.shootforpar.com

Amateurs can get tips and advice at this site.

143

The University of Golf

http://www.golfuniversity.com

Enjoy matriculating here. This University will teach you the secrets of a better golf game.

144
Inner What!

http://www.innergolf.com

For those who feel that the game is mostly mental.

145
Get Psyched!

http://www.golfpsych.com

Here's a system that evaluates your personality, compares it to the champion pros and advises how to emulate them.

146
Peak Performance

http://www.peaksports.com

How many times have you said, "Golf is all mental?" Well, here are the answers to the mental aspects of the game.

"Sure you can see your doctor. That's him on the ninth tee."

147
Fit for Golf
http://www.simplefitnesssolutions.com/products/golf.htm
Play better by getting in shape.

148
Tips for Seniors
http://hometown.aol.com/golf4srs/index.html
Join the senior tour on the Net. Tips, jokes and more are here.

149
It's a Trick
http://www.golftrickshots.com
Paul Hahn will show you some trick shots.

150

Break 100

http://www.golfschoolonline.com
Here's a site for beginners, juniors and golfers who can't break 100.

151

Join the Academy

http://www.golfacademy.com
http://www.golfspan.com
Need some instructions? Get them online. Tell them what ails you, and they'll give you the fix.

152

The Perfect Swing

http://members.aol.com/beau1943/golfswings/golf.htm
View the pros, and then aspire to the perfect swing.

153
Back to School
http://www.thegolfschool.com
Here's the Web site for the "Original" Golf School — with seven locations around the country.

154
The Academy of Golf
http://www.pgagolfacademy.com
Go to PGA National Resort & Spa to learn more about playing golf.

155
Teach Me Golf
http://www.learningvacations.com/golf.htm
Book a "learning vacation" at any of the golf schools listed here.

156
Golf 101

http://www.golf101.com
New to the game of golf? Take some lessons at this site.

157
Give Me a Tip

http://www.CyberTip4theDay.com
All of us need some improvement. Get a daily golf tip e-mailed to you.

158
Golf Score Tracker

http://www.golftracker.com
Document your scores here. And if you happen to be proud of a particular score, e-mail it to someone you know.

159
Your Own Green

http://www.tourtrue.com

An effective short game practice area can be built in as little as three hundred square feet of space in your yard.

160
Train Me, Please

http://www.golftrainingaids.com

Check out these golf-training aids to improve your game.

161
Let's Be Honest

http://www.tqs.net

Track your scores with this golfer's diary.

162
I Love School

http://www.golfschoolinfo.com

The Golf School is a directory of schools around the country. You might want to enroll and shave a few strokes off your score.

CHAPTER VII
ON THE ROAD

163
Travelin'

http://expedia.msn.com
http://www.travelweb.com
http://www.travelocity.com
These are a few of the superior travel sites on the Net. Use them to help with your golf-related — or general — travel plans.

164
Travel Scorecard

http://www.gomez.com
Here's a different type of scorecard. Let Gomez tell you about the best travel sites on the Net.

165
Resort Time

http://www.resortgolfcourses.com
Search for resort golf courses.

166
Golf Direct

http://www.golfdirect.com
Go directly to this site to find out about golf resorts, communities, vacations and more.

167
Rooms and Golf

http://www.roomsplus.com
Need a place to stay when playing golf out of town? Rooms Plus has that information for you.

168
Scotland

http://www.scotlandgolf.com

http://www.scotlands-golf-courses.com

These sites will get you close to the green grass of Scotland.

169
Travel and Leisure—Golf

http://www.tlgolf.com

Check out Travel and Leisure's excellent golf magazine.

170
Golf.com Travels

http://www.golf.com/trav

This major golf site on the Net provides you with travel tips and information.

171
Where to Stay and Play
http://www.globalgolf.com
Golfers can view the courses, book tee times, choose accommodations and learn about restaurants and places of interest.

172
The World's Best Courses
http://www.concierge.com/travel/g_cnt/04_features/golf99/intro.html
Let some experts help you identify the greatest courses.

173
Golf Resorts
http://www.resort-golf.com
Going on vacation? Check out these resorts.

174
Resorts Online
http://www.resortsonline.com/golf
Let these sites lend a hand in finding the perfect resort for you.

175
Romantic Golf
http://www.aaacom.com/golf/welcomee.htm
How about playing a round or two in the French Riviera?

176
Just One More Round
http://www.pgatravel.com
Let Pacific Golf Adventures assist in planning your golf vacation.

177
Match Travel
http://www.golfcircuit.com/travel
Match your golf travel needs with resorts in the U.S., Mexico and Caribbean.

178
Register Now
http://www.registryone.com
If you are searching for a home in a club setting with golf and other amenities, register here.

179
Virtual Guide
http://www.globalgolfguide.com
Take a virtual tour of some magnificent courses throughout the world.

180
Mountain Golf
http://www.greatsmokiesgolf.com
http://www.smokymtns.com/golf.htm
Play a round in the Great Smoky Mountains.

181
Sunshine Golfing
http://www.floridagolfing.com
Tee it up in the Sunshine State.

182
California Dreaming
http://www.golfcalifornia.com
Go west, young man—not bad advice for any golfer.

183
Hey Cowboy

http://www.golfsw.com
Golf Texas style.

184
Going to Disney?

http://www.grandcypress.com
If you want to treat yourself to fine golf and accommodations, stay at this grand place.

185
Pebble Beach

http://www.pebblebeach.com
With green fees there of $275, you might want to save up before going to play.

186
Pinehurst, North Carolina
http://www.pinehurst.com
Visit one of golf's most famous resorts. Eight courses are waiting for you.

187
Palm Springs
http://www.palmsprings.com/golf.html
One of the greatest places to play golf.

188
Rocky Mountain High
http://www.rockiesgolf.com
http://www.golfcolorado.com
Check out this golf site dedicated to playing in the Rockies.

189
Golf Utah
http://www.rockiesgolf.com/utah
Once in these beautiful mountains, you may never want to play at home again.

190
Golf Arizona
http://www.cactusgolf.com
Desert golf: fun in the sun.

191
Southern Hospitality
http://www.southerngolf.com
Southern golf meets the Internet.

192
Golfing in South Carolina

http://www.golfdesk.com
http://www.navi-gator.com
http://www.golfholiday.com
http://www.myrtlebeachgolf.com
http://www.myrtlebeach-info.com
http://www.travelsc.com/thingstodo/golf/home.html
Some of the golf meccas of the world: Myrtle Beach, Hilton Head, Charleston and many more fine courses.

193
Golf Hawaii

http://www.golfkona.com
http://www.islandgolf.com
Play a little golf in our fiftieth state. Watch out for the water hazards.

194
North of the Border
http://www.canadagolf.com

If you want to know about playing in Canada, check it out.

195
Golfing BC
http://www.golfbc.com

Get details about playing in British Columbia.

196
O Canada!
http://www.scoregolf.com

Here is Canada's number one golf site and magazine on the Net.

197
Aim for the Stick

http://www.flagstick.com
http://www.ontariogolf.com
Flagstick magazine serves the Ontario area, but there is good information for those in the U.S. as well.

198
Tee It Up in Montreal

http://www.golfmontreal.com
One of the world's great cities also has great golf.

199
Golf Europe

http://www.golfeurope.com
If your plans include playing on other continents, check out this European site.

200
Playing Down Under

http://www.golf.com.au
Learn how to arrange playing golf in Australia.

201
Everything Asian

http://www.asiangolf.com
Golf Asian style.

202
Golf en Espagne

http://www.golfinspain.com
The ball in Spain falls mainly on the green.

203
Golfing Safari
http://www.kenya-golf-safaris.com
Watch out for lions, elephants and the rest of the wild kingdom in Africa.

204
U.K. Golf
http://www.uk-golf.com
Golfing in Britain? Hit this site first.

205
Golf Today
http://www.golftoday.co.uk
Europe's premier online golf magazine.

206
Golf Outing

http://www.johnnyjet.com

Planning a golf trip? Here's a good place to start.

207
Luck of the Irish

http://www.irishgolf.com

http://www.golfingireland.com

http://www.golfclubireland.com

http://www.golfing-ireland.com

Need information about some of the great places to play a round in Ireland? Good luck playing these challenging courses.

208
Golf in Thailand

http://www.golfinthailand.com

No matter where you go on this planet, golf courses are waiting for you.

209
Golf Turkey

http://www.golfturkey.com

This has nothing to do with Thanksgiving. If you want to play golf in Turkey, here's the Web site to make the arrangements.

210
Ship 'em

http://www.golfbagshipping.com

Admit it, you're tired of carrying your golf clubs on the plane. Let these folks ship them for you.

211
Driving?

http://www.freetrip.com
No not from the tee box. If you're driving out of town on your golf vacation, use this site to get free directions.

212
Show Me the Way

http://www.zip2.com
If you're invited to play at a course you have never been to, use this site to get door-to-door directions.

213
Golf's a Blast

http://www.mapblast.com

Need to find a golf course or a golf-related store? Mapblast asks for your location and then provides tons of good resources for you, including detailed directions.

CHAPTER VIII
YOU BELONG TO ME

214
United States Golf Association

http://www.usga.org

http://www.usga.org/rules

Need to know the rules and more? Make a visit to the USGA site.

215
The Governing Authority

http://www.randa.org

The Royal and Ancient Golf Club of St. Andrews is the governing authority for golf…not including Canada and the United States.

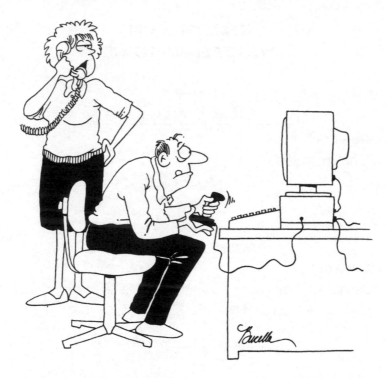

"Can he call you back? He's putting right now."

216
Hey, Southpaw!
http://www.nalg.org
It's the National Association of Left-Handed Golfers.

217
U.S. National Senior Open Golf Association
http://www.usnseniorsgolf.org
This association was formed to unite professional and amateur golfers in the interest and promotion of seniors golf competition on a national basis and to engender between both groups a close, friendly and lasting relationship.

218
Single Digits
http://www.singlesgolf.com
This site proclaims: "The perfect blend of fun, fellowship and fairways — singles meeting singles through golf."

219
Royal Canadian Golf Association

http://www.rcga.org

Lots of interesting golf information and resources from Canada.

220
Golf for Everyone

http://www.mgaa.com

The Minority Golf Association of America is trying to make this a reality.

221
Multicultural Golf

http://www.minoritygolf.com

Locate information on minority golf, junior golf and other events around the country. Click on buttons to learn more about this association.

222
African-American Golf Association
http://www.aaga.com

The AAGA promotes the enjoyment of golf among African-Americans.

223
National Foundation of Golf
http://www.ngf.org

Its mission is "to foster the growth and economic vitality of golf."

224
Future Great Ones — Male
http://www.ncaachampionships.com/gol/mgol/index.html

Preview the future greats of the PGA Tour.

225
The College Golf Foundation

http://www.cgfgolf.org
The foundation is dedicated to the growth and promotion of men's and women's collegiate golf.

226
Future Great Ones—Female

http://www.ncaachampionships.com/gol/wgol/index.html
Preview the future greats of the LPGA Tour.

227
Professional Clubmakers' Society

http://www.proclubmakers.org
The people who manufacture the clubs.

228
Golf Course Superintendent Association

http://www.gcsaa.org
The guys who maintain the courses.

229
American Junior Golf Association

http://www.ajga.org
Dedicated to the development of young men and women through competitive junior golf.

230
CPGA

http://www.canadianpgaatlantic.org
It's the Canadian Professional Golfer's Association.

231
What Makes a Golf Hole Great?

http://www.golfdesign.org

Let the American Society of Golf Course Architects tell you.

232
American Amateur Cybergolf Association

http://www.aacga.com

AACGA is designed by amateurs for amateur golfers. Get involved with its regularly scheduled tournaments.

233
Wanna Teach?

http://www.pgtaa.com

If you have aspirations of becoming a golf instructor, visit the Professional Golf Teachers Association of America.

234
Golf Trade

http://www.golftrade.com

If you work in the golf industry, this site can provide some helpful information.

235
What's Your Handicap?

http://www.golf-handicap.com

Check out what The International Golf Handicap Service has to offer.

236
Link Me Up

http://www.golflink.net

Here is information on golf associations, courses, manufacturers, merchandise, pro shops, real estate, resorts, schools, tips and travel.

237
Tournament Time

http://www.nagtd.com

Do you ever attend or sponsor golf tournaments? If you do, you may want to visit with The National Association of Golf Tournament Directors.

CHAPTER IX
I'LL BUY THAT

238
Gotta Big Head?

http://www.lynxgolf.com

http://www.pinggolf.com

http://www.cobragolf.com

http://www.callawaygolf.com

http://www.clevelandgolf.com

http://www.taylormadegolf.com

http://www.golfonline.com/links/equipment.html

These golf club industry leaders are eager to show you their products.

239
Taylor Made for Kids
http://www.taylormadekids.com
Taylor Made wants to get 'em (into golf) while they're young.

240
Build It Yourself
http://www.rangergolf.com
Build your own custom clubs online.

241
Let it Fly

http://www.maxfli.com
http://www.topflite.com
http://www.titleist.com
Which ball do you prefer?

242
Walk Softly…

http://www.softspikes.com
Softspikes is the pioneer of alternative golf cleats, spearheading the effort to ban metal spikes from courses.

243
It's a Dogleg

http://www.doglegsportswear.com
How many times have you used that expression? It's about time you wear it!

244
I'll Bid

http://auction.amazon.com
http://auctions.yahoo.com/25042-category.html
Go to these auction sites and bid whatever you like for golf equipment.

245
Golf Bay

http://www.ebay.com
Ebay is the famous Internet auction company. Just type "golf" in the search box and you will be able to bid on thousands of golf items.

246
Buy It Online

http://www.fogdog.com
Golfers buy a lot of gear, and this is their shop on the Net.

247
Ashworth

http://www.ashworthinc.com
When it comes to branding, these guys have the name.

248
Shop Online
http://www.golfshoponline.com
Some cool golf items for those who love the game.

249
Golf Store
http://www.thesportsstore.com
This store has tons of golf stuff for you.

250
Buy Golf
http://onlinesports.com/pages/top,sprt,golf.html
Online Sports has a variety of golf items to purchase.

"Golf? Well, Arlene's been on my back all day
about cleaning the attic..."

251
Mammoth Golf
http://www.mammothgolf.com
A superstore that has most of the items that golfers purchase.

252
Discount Golf Superstore
http://www.golfdiscount.com
This one claims to be "your Internet source to the lowest prices on the best names in golf."

253
Chip Shot Golf
http://www.chipshot.com
Claims to be "the Internet's largest retailer of custom-built golf equipment."

254
Watt's in This Store?
http://www.edwinwatts.com
All of your golf needs.

255
Imprint This!
http://www.pargolf.com
Got a golf item you want imprinted? Pargolf has if for you.

256
The Gift of Golf
http://www.ticketslive.com/csigolf.html
Give a round of golf as a gift.

257
Gift Collection

http://www.golfcollection.com

Can't find the perfect gift item for the golfer in your life? Try the Golf Collection site.

258
Classic Gifts

http://www.classicgolfgifts.com

All golfers love golf-related gifts. You can find many at this site.

259
Great Moments in Golf

http://www.webshots.com

Get your golf screen savers here.

260
Art and Golf

http://www.artistsgolf.com
Take a look at some of these famous courses through the eyes of some famous artists.

261
Art Golf

http://www.golf-art.com
Liven up your living room or boardroom with these magnificent paintings.

262
The Art of Golf

http://golf-arts.com
Need a special gift? Let Donna Hollingsworth create a custom portrait of you on your favorite hole.

263
Monitor This
http://www.golfmonitor.com
This site tracks golf products, specials and reviews.

264
I'm a Golf Great
http://www.rwga.com/weall1f.htm
Get your picture painted in a collage with other greats.

265
Golfing Books
http://www.golfingbooks.com
Find good prices on all golf books.

266
Good Night
http://www.cnisbelieving.com
Play golf at night with these products.

267
Want a Ride?
http://www.acegolfcarsplace.com
Lots of cool golf carts at this site.

268
Iron Out a Deal
http://www.golfclubexchange.com
You can buy, sell or trade your clubs at the exchange.

269
Line Drive Fishing
http://www.smartbiz.org/linedrive
Combine your love of fishing and golf by doing both at the same time.

270
Golfer Want a Cookie?
http://www.womengolfers.com/cookies.htm
Let the ladies from Womengolfers.com provide you with golf cookies.

271
Golf Reviewer
http://www.golfreview.net
Product reviews by consumers for consumers.

CHAPTER X
TRADITION!

272
Old Wood

http://www.oldcourse.com
Dedicated to the history of golf equipment.

273
Golf Museum

http://www.golfmuseum.com
Visit the Philadelphia Private Golf Museum site. For only four million dollars, you can buy the entire collection.

274
Clubs and Collectibles
http://www.solu.net/barry

http://www.golfforallages.com

Make a visit and see pictures of some old golf items available for purchase.

275
Golf History
http://www.geocities.com/Augusta/1525

If you want to combine golf with U.S. history, check out Colonial Williamsburg.

276
Golf Collectors Society
http://www.golfcollectors.com

Preserving the tradition and treasures of the game of golf.

277
Tradition!

http://www.oldgolf.com

Here's the history of golf.

CHAPTER XI
EQUAL PLAY

278
Women's Golf
http://womensgolf.about.com
http://www.womensgolftoday.com
Women also love golf.

279
Women's Golf Catalog
http://www.womensgolf.com
Thousands of products for the female golfer.

280
More for the Ladies
http://www.womengolfers.com
The Web site by, for and about women golfers.

281
Kids Golf

http://www.kidsgolf.com

Enter your child in the "Drive, Pitch & Putt" National Junior Skills Challenge.

282
Start 'em Young

http://www.teachkidsgolf.com

Here's an all-in-one book and video to teach kids from age two to twelve.

283
Senior Golfer

http://www.seniorgolfer.com

The magazine dedicated to…senior golfers.

CHAPTER XII
LINKS ABOUT THE LINKS

284
Join the Tour

http://www.etour.com

Join this tour and you'll find hand-selected golf sites for your surfing pleasure.

285
The 19th Hole

http://www.19thhole.com

There is a lot of good information at this site, cocktails not included.

286
It's Free

http://www.freegolfinfo.com

Learn about a lot of free golf stuff on the Internet.

287
Golf Search

http://www.golfsearch.com

Sorry, this site will not find your lost ball, but it will tell you where to find golf-related items on the Net.

288
Universal Links

http://www.websbestgolflinks.com

This site has hundreds of links to golf resources.

289
Everything Golf

http://www.ttsoft.com/thor/golflinks.html

Check out Thor's links to golf-related sites.

290
Only the Best Links

http://www.bestcoursestoplay.com

Here are links to the best daily fee and resort courses.

291
Bytes as Links

http://www.golfbytes.com

Golf Bytes has over 2,000 golf sites.

292
Golf Life

http://www.golfclubs.com

This link-loaded site states that "Golf is not just a sport…it's a lifestyle."

293
Net Caddie
http://www.netcaddie.com/links/index.htm
This caddie has spotted many good sites for you on the Net.

294
Discover This
http://www.sports.sleuth.com
Consider this sleuth your friend; it will find all kinds of timely golf information for you.

295
Links and Hyperlinks
http://www.duffer.com
Includes a complete search engine with "more golf links than Yahoo!"

296
In Search of Golf

http://www.golfsearchengine.com
Take a swing at this search engine. It's guaranteed to set you straight.

297
Link Mania

http://www.golflinkmania.com
From books to many links, you'll find them here.

298
PuttLinks

http://pga.fantasyteam.com/puttlinks
Get linked up to pictures, rules, organizations and more.

299
Lookin' Smart

http://www.looksmart.com
LookSmart has a lot of great stuff at its site. Make sure you click on Sports and Recreation and you will be sent to many good golf sites.

300
Search the Net

http://www.altavista.com
http://www.yahoo.com
http://www.hotbot.com
http://www.excite.com
http://www.lycos.com
There are certainly a few more golf sites that are worth visiting, so use these incredible search engines to find them. A recent search for "golf" at Altavista reveals 7,903,404 matches found. Happy surfing!

INDEX (BY SITE NUMBER)

Index (by Site Number)

INDEX (BY SITE NUMBER)

The Incredible Newsletter

If you are enjoying this book, you can also arrange to receive a steady stream of more "incredible Internet things," delivered directly to your e-mail address.

The Leebow Letter, Ken Leebow's weekly e-mail newsletter, provides new sites, updates on existing ones and information about other happenings on the Internet.

For more details about *The Leebow Letter* and how to subscribe, visit us at:

WWW.300INCREDIBLE.COM

(USO) United Service Organizations

For nearly 60 years, the United Service Organizations (USO) has "Delivered America" to service members stationed around the world, thousands of miles from family and friends. The USO provides celebrity entertainment, recreation, cultural orientation, language training, travel assistance, telephone and Internet access, and other vital services to military personnel and their families at 115 locations worldwide. The USO is a non-profit organization, not a government agency. It relies on the generosity of corporations and individuals to enable its programs and services to continue. For more information on contributing to the USO, please call 1-800-876-7469 or visit its Web site at www.uso.org.